I0478775

Blockchain

Innovative and Modern Financial Framework that will revolutionize the Next Digital Economy with Blockchain Technology

Series: Hacking Freedom and Data Freedom (Blockchain Edition)

By Isaac D. Cody

BLOCKCHAIN TECHNOLOGY

INNOVATIVE AND MODERN FINANCIAL FRAMEWORK THAT WILL REVOLUTIONIZE THE NEXT DIGITAL ECONOMY WITH BLOCKCHAIN TECHNOLOGY

ISAAC D. CODY

Table of Contents

Conclusion and Resources

Related Titles

Introduction

Blockchain technology is, perhaps, as firmly and unequivocally believed by many technological experts to be the next best thing in their world after the Internet. Just like the Internet, it is not necessary for you to know what Blockchain technology is and how it works for you to use it. However, it is always better to have a basic idea about these things so that you can understand its revolutionary nature. Hence, I thought it makes sense to give you a sound understanding about the basics of this technology so that you are intrigued enough to delve deeper and learn more about it.

So What Is It Exactly?

So, what is blockchain technology?
Imagine a shared spreadsheet that is duplicated and is available to access by an entire network of computers. Next, think of this spreadsheet being updated regularly by this network of computers. This is the basic foundation of a blockchain. The data on a blockchain is not held by any one computer but is shared by all who access it. It is being *continuously* reconciled. Think bigger. Imagine tens, hundreds, thousands, and even

millions of computers and people all in this network, updating it's data and contents to provide anyone access to it. While the availability of this shared data is outstanding, it is shortening the gap of communication and access to one another in an amazing and profound way.

The fact that the data is not stored at any one location makes it easily verifiable and makes it truly public. No hacker will be able to corrupt the data as it is not centrally stored anywhere. As it is used by millions of computing devices across the world, it is easily accessible to anyone on the Internet.

The power of blockchain technology is here and boy, I guarantee you this popularity will explode within the next 5-10 years. It's already becoming mainstream and while you sleep, the networks interwoven in its system is ready to take off.

Use Google Sheet Times A Million

William Mougayar, a blockchain specialist, uses Google Docs as an analogy to explain blockchain. Here is a summary of what he says. Suppose, you needed a document you have created to be revised by another team member. You would send the document to him or her and ask him to read it and make any revisions.

In the meantime, if you wanted to make any changes to the document yourself, you would not be able to make them, as you will have to first wait for the other person to get back with the changes. This is the old concept of collaboration where you have to wait your turn before you choose to make changes or add anything to a document or spreadsheet or anything else. Nobody likes taking turns. If this system in place is repeated, the finality of that spreadsheet will take days, or even weeks to finish depending on what the content is. Who knew "taking turns" was such as a hassle. That is no longer an issue with Blockchain Technology.

Now back to the example, if you were to use Google Docs, you would save a document onto the cloud and make it available to all the members of your team. Each of you could make changes or edit the document and the changes are updated immediately so that the next person who views it has the latest updated version. Although you do not need a blockchain for editing and accessing documents, Google Docs is a powerful analogy to illustrate the way a blockchain works.

Breakdown It to Block and Chain

All users at all points of times can access Blockchain and the latest updated version is available to everyone at the same time. Another way of thinking about this is examining the actual word of Blockchain. Each "block" is like the contents of which the user has. Each user has information and data tethered to it (a "chain") and that chain is attached to other blocks. Other chains are attached to it and everyone has access to that same "chain" of information. Now multiply it by millions and you get something that will revolutionize the world when it comes to information processing.

So, to summarize, a "Blockchain" is a series of information and data that is public, easily accessible to Internet users, and does not have a central storage location. It is a distributed database that is safe from marauding hackers and yet has the power to make a legal monetary transaction without fear of frauds and thefts.

Initially, blockchain technology was devised specifically for digital monetary transactions. The first currency of blockchain technology is called bitcoin in the financial world. However, this technology has found many applications across other platforms as well including social media, digital banking, etc. So, read on and find out more about Blockchain technology and how you can harness its power.

Chapter 1: History of Blockchain Technology and Unraveling the Blockchain

Any new subject, I personally believe, has a deeper meaning to the learner when he or she goes right back to the first known origins. Hence, I chose to include a bit of history of the Blockchain technology before we move on to understanding it better.

The History Of The Blockchain Technology

The word "Blockchain" was used for the first time in Bitcoin's original source code. Although today, Bitcoin and Blockchain technology are separated, the histories of both the concepts have the same origins. And hence, it makes sense to study the histories of these two together.

Bitcoin is actually a virtual currency. In October 2008, the Bitcoin was invented by an anonymous person(s) known as Satoshi Nakamoto. The identity of the original source code writer(s) is still a mystery although several theories and counter-theories that prove/disprove this identity are extant.

In January 2009, the source code was released as open source when Satoshi Nakamoto "mined" (more about mining and miners later) the first Bitcoins and started the Bitcoin network. In April 2011, Satoshi Nakamoto vanished from the bitcoin scenario and the alias did not appear in any of the Bitcoin papers or forums. In fact, the alias did not even contribute to the code anymore after this time.

Despite the disappearance of the founding member(s), Bitcoin technology continues to flourish and the community is continuously working on addressing various issues right up to today's date. In fact, there was a rather serious threat to the technology in April 2013, when a fork appeared in the Bitcoin Blockchain. This resulted in Bitcoin values plummeting as owners scrambled to sell what they had. However, developers and the Bitcoin community worked hard to rectify this technical glitch and soon, Bitcoins were back on track. The issue was resolved and sorted out satisfactorily by the Bitcoin community.

After this glitch was rectified, Bitcoin technology actually took off. More websites and online stores started accepting Bitcoin currency and investors too started betting on Bitcoin-based startups. In 2013, the value of a Bitcoin reached an all-time high of $1108 driven by demand and the increasing investments in this technology.

As bitcoin technology gained in popularity, it also attracted more scrutiny from law enforcement agencies. In 2013, nearly 70% of bitcoin transactions of the world were being handled out of Mt. Gox Bitcoin exchange and this was shut down by the Department of Homeland Security. There were reports that nearly 744, 000 Bitcoins were stolen from Mt. Gox and amidst these negative reports, this exchange filed for bankruptcy.

Today, the value of a Bitcoin currency is approximately $415. Additionally, other currencies such as Dogecoin and Litecoin have also been developed using the Blockchain technology of Bitcoins. However, these currencies have not gained as much popularity as Bitcoins primarily because users and investors are wary of the volatility of both the community and the codes involved. Even Bitcoins are losing their sheen and economic and finance pundits are warning people of its uncertainty.

However, it must be kept in mind that Blockchain technology-based Bitcoin codes are in a very nascent stage and writing them off completely would be rather foolhardy. Yes, these concepts are still evolving and its deployment in sensitive areas like finance and banking will be vulnerable to various issues, frailties and hugely differing opinions.

Although the popularity of Bitcoins are appearing to be on the wane despite government organizations and banks showing sufficient interest in the technology, Blockchain technology is becoming more popular as it finds applications in different segments of human life.

Unraveling The BlockChain

Like I said in the introduction, the Blockchain is a shared and distributed database available in innumerable copies across a wide and huge network of computers. Allow me to expand a little more about this.

Satoshi Nakamoto did not "create" any new inventions when inventing blockchain. Satoshi Nakamoto is credited with having combined existing computing ideas such as Proof-of-work algorithm, cryptographic signatures, and Merkle chains to work in a peer-to-peer computer network to create a distributed trustless consensus system. (more on this in the next chapter)

Any transaction on the Blockchain requires a digital signature for authentication that is based on public key cryptography. This digital signature has two keys, a public key and a private key. These two keys are mathematically related to each other in such a complex way that it is computationally unfeasible to make any sort of a guess.

The public key is sent specifically to a designated receiver and only this designated receiver can decrypt this key using his or her private key. Public key cryptography allows you to encrypt messages and also allows you to authenticate a message or transaction in such a way that the receiver can verify if it has been altered at any time during the transaction. Or rather, if any change happens, the receiver will be able to make out that changes have happened.

Got all that?

As the Blockchain is copied multiple times in multiple computing devices, any new transaction must also be sent to all the computing nodes of the network so that the Blockchain remains in sync throughout the range of users and the ledger remains one "worldwide ledger" that is updated at all the computing devices. This is an essential part of the Blockchain which, if not done, will result in multiple and conflicting ledgers in the computers of the different users.

This, essentially, translates to a process that updates all the distributed copies so that they are reconciled to include the new transaction and all the users have access to the same version of the Blockchain. This process happens via a consensus mode wherein a majority of the nodes must accept the new transaction for it to be a valid one and be included in the blockchain.

Consensus

This consensus process of approval of a new transaction is one of the most important aspects of Blockchain technology. This consensus happens on an "emergent" basis and not during any fixed interval or time. It happens as and when a new transaction takes place on the Blockchain or when a new block is added to the chain. So, now we go to understanding "What is a block?" in a blockchain? The next chapter talks in detail about the blocks in a blockchain.

Chapter 2: Blocks In A Blockchain

Blockchains, as can be logically understood, consist of blocks that are verified and authenticated computationally before being added onto the chain. Each block has the following parts:

- A list of transactions

- A block header

Each block header, in turn, has at least the following 3 sets of metadata:

- Information regarding the transactions that are in the block

- The data and the timestamp regarding proof-of-work algorithm

- A "hash" reference to the parent block (or the preceding block)

What Is A Proof-Of-Work Algorithm?

Proof of work is a prerequisite that is performed through complex computations so that the block or transaction is understood to be verified and authenticated for adding to the blockchain.

As explained in the previous chapter, the idea of Proof of work (POW) existed even before Satoshi Nakamoto. However, the credit for innovation of the Bockchain technology (first used in Bitcoins) goes to Satoshi Nakamoto because of his (or their or her) skill to combine POW with other existing ideas such as Merkle chains, cryptographic signatures, and P2P networks to arrive at a feasible distributed consensus system without the fear of loss of trust (or trustless)

So, now let's go further and understand POW in Blockchain technology. POW requires extremely high levels of computation powers that are normally found only in really expensive computers. So, to understand how Blockchain technology works, we must clearly understand how this distributed trustless consensus works. So, there are three words to understand here namely *consensus*, *distributed* and *trustless*.

Consensus – The common understanding of reaching a consensus is that wherein all the concerned people in a group agree on something, be it an action to be taken or the outcome to be achieved or a leader to be chosen amongst themselves etc.

In the realm of a language, consensus means that people talking the same language understand that when X is said, then it means Y. For example, at the dinner table, when you ask your spouse to "pass the salt," your spouse understands that you want to get the salt and you understand that your spouse understands this. Suppose you were in a country whose language you did not know. Then, you'd perhaps not use "pass the salt." You would use pointing a finger or some other action, so that you know for sure the person you are talking to understands what you want. "Consensus" is thus also what is normally termed as "common knowledge."

With the concept of money, consensus must include an understanding of the transaction by the parties directly involved and also the rest of the society. For example, if I have received a certain currency from someone, the rest of the people in the place I come from should accept this currency to be valid and recognize its value.

Hence, I will accept a process in payment or token of payment if it meets the following criteria:

- It should come from a scarce source of supply *using an accepted form of value* creation and/or exchange. For example, frogs cannot be used as currency as this is easily guessable. You cannot simply draw your national flag on a piece of paper and expect to get currency value for it because it is not an accepted form of value creation or exchange.

- *Everyone should accept this token or process as currency of comparable value*

- Everyone else should necessarily stick to the first two rules

While this may appear very simplistic, it is the most basic and core aspect of finance and money. With this understanding of consensus about currency, we move on to "distributed."

Distributed – This means that the data is not held in one central location but, multiple copies are held on all the networked computers or nodes. The trick about distribution in Blockchain technology is the question of how to ensure there is consistency of data in the system. This means when one node makes a change, then this change must be reflected in every computer or that node that holds a copy of the Blockchain.

There are two ways to manage this data consistency. The first method, also called *strict consistency*, is by slowing down the things until such time has passed that the data is correctly reflected everywhere.

The second method (a slightly unreliable way), also referred to as *eventual consistency* is to accept the transaction as authentic but hold the right to withdraw in case of a potential conflict later on.

Trustless – Trust is an implicit agreement in digital banking today. There is something called "trust of safety" which you place on the entity that is holding your account information that it will not go debiting your account without your approval.

There is the "trust of issuance" which you place on the same entity that it will not assign itself money that is actually yours.

Then, there is the "trust of correctness" which you place on the entity's system that it will do its job correctly and ensure consistency of your currency data.

Then, what did Satoshi Nakamoto mean by trustless? This simply means that we do not need to depend on the malicious or bona fide intentions of any particular party to carry out our transactions. And the answer to this question of trust is given by *cryptographic signatures*.

If all the people present in the system can decline to accept a transaction without a cryptographic signature and can easily verify an authentic signature, then the question of having to trust anyone becomes redundant.

This means that no one else except you can do transactions with your currency.
So, for a monetary transaction to work using Blockchain technology, the following criteria would have to be met:

• The person who is originating the transaction must have the required funds in his or her possession

• The person should have received the funds by a transaction that is commonly accepted as valid

• When the transaction is complete, the receiver of the funds will be recognized as having got the funds.

- When the transaction is complete, the originator will not be able to use those transferred funds any more

Any user will use a specific algorithm that combines all the above-described criteria so that the transaction block becomes authentic.

Example Time!

Let me give you an example. An algorithm could include a cryptographic signature for verification of the transaction. And the above 4 criteria combined together to form an algorithm can be true and valid only with the user's knowledge and approval. Thus, the chances for duplication or fraud are not computationally feasible.

That is how blocks are created, mined, and then added to a Blockchain that is distributed across all the copies held at all the nodes.

In summary, Blockchain technology has the following five key components:

Decentralized consensus – This concept brings about a paradigm shift from a present state where a centralized database is used to validate a transaction. A decentralized system transfers the trust and the authority to virtual network that is decentralized and enables connected nodes or computers to continuously record transactions through public blocks that form a Blockchain. Every block contains a unique fingerprint through the use of unique "hashes" or verification codes that are computationally unfeasible to duplicate. And it is important to remember here that the consensus and the application itself are separate from each other and hence applications can be written for both money and non-money applications.

The Blockchain – A blockchain is a public place where you store data in a container (or block). While the block itself can be seen by all, the contents of the block are visible only to the recipient and the originator because only they hold the respective private key needed to authenticate the transaction. So, the blocks on the blockchain have public visibility but with private inspection rights. A good analogy would be your home. Your home address is publicly available to all. But, the access to enter your home is only with you and nobody can get in until you approve.

Smart Contracts – This is a small program that is built around a currency value and is governed by a set of rules and regulations. This format of governance is verifiable through computation and does not need any arbitrator or gatekeeper to manage and keep a check on the authenticity of these contracts. The core principle behind the concept of smart contracts is that there is *no need for an external arbitrator when the related parties of a transaction are willing to get into an agreement by themselves.*

The relevant parties agree on the rules to be followed and use computational algorithms to verify the authenticity of the contract. These algorithms are verifiable through self-managed computer nodes that are connected via a network. Each contract belongs to a particular owner and is linked to the Blockchain.

Trustless transactions (or trusted computation) – The combination of Blockchain technology, smart contracts, and decentralized consensus enables transactions and resources to be verified computationally between peer-to-peer computers at a much deeper level making it unfeasible for any kind of human intervention with mala fide intent.

Each Blockchain is the unbiased validator of all the transactions (or blocks). The rules of contracts, governance, agreements and law are all technology-based and hence free from potential frauds that could linger in the minds of human beings. Hence, transactions via Blockchain technology are considered "trustless" transactions.

Proof of work – The central governing theme of Blockchain technology is the proof of the work or proof of stake that forms the ultimate authenticator of all transactions or blocks in the Blockchain. This proof of work (which is embedded in the unique hash) gives you the "right" to take part in the transaction through creation of blocks that will ultimately become part of the Blockchain.

This proof of work is a "huge hurdle" that is computationally unfeasible to change or hack into without leaving a trail of the changes. Any small change in the record will result in a new proof of work enabling the receiver of the block or transaction to identify and recognize fraudulent transactions or blocks. As of now, proof of work is the most expensive aspect of Blockchain technology and is, perhaps, the most limiting factor in this realm. But more about limitations later on!

Chapter 3: Cryptocurrency And Bitcoin

Let us start understand Blockchain technology by learning how it is applied in different fields. This chapter is dedicated to cryptocurrency.

Many average non-technological people look at cryptocurrency like it was a character from a fairy tale, which really does not exist. Like the unicorn, perhaps? So, this chapter will help you understand whether cryptocurrency is really only a unicorn or the money of the future.

Although cryptocurrency is still geeky to many people around the world, most of them are aware of its existence. Even large corporate houses, banks and the government too are not fully aware of the potential of cryptocurrency to change the way we do financial business.

Yet, development work and research work is underway with many large banks and other financial institutions as well as large companies and the government working and conducting research in the realm of cryptocurrency. Many banks have invested money to start some kind of blockchain project even if the work is still in the nascent stages.

By now, I have already explained in the previous that cryptocurrency is a by-product of Satoshi Nakamoto's blockchain technology.

In fact, cryptocurrency is the first application of blockchain technology. When Satoshi Nakamoto announced the first cryptocurrency "bitcoin" in 2008, he said that he had developed a "peer-to-peer (P2P) electronic cash system."

Until then, many people had attempted to build digital cash systems and had failed and Satoshi Nakamoto is credited with creating a digital system that is feasible and scalable too.

The basis of any payment system consists of transactions, balances and accounts. Most payment systems work with the central theme of ensuring that money does not get doubly credited or doubly spent. That means to say, if you have used an amount from your balance, then that amount should not be available to you for use. Traditionally, and to this day, this is managed by keeping a centralized database of all accounts and balances through which the payment system is routed and transactions are carried out.

So, when you make a payment from the balance in your account, the central database is accessed. The relevant amount is debited from your account and a new reduced balance is reflected in it. Then the amount is transferred to the recipient. Thus, balances and accounts are centrally controlled. We have already spoken about the three trust elements that are essential in managing and running this kind of financial environment. Let me summarize quickly again to enhance your understanding of how cryptocurrency works in contrast to this concept of "trust."

The three trust elements in any financial system include:

Trust of safety – the trust that you, as an account holder, place on the entity controlling the centralized database for safeguarding your accounts and balances from mala fide use is called the trust of safety.

Trust of issuance – The trust that you place on this same controlling entity that it will not take away your balance for itself arbitrarily and will issue payments based only on your authorization is called the trust of issuance.

Trust of correctness – The trust you place on the system that is maintained and managed by the centralized database controlling entity that it is performing its functions correctly and without errors based on your instructions.

In a network that is decentralized, there is no server. So, every entity in the network will have to do the functions. Every peer who is part of the network will have to update its copy of the Blockchain so that it can carry out valid transactions in the future that will be accepted by all the other peers of the network.

For this, you have to achieve consensus regarding the transactions in the Blockchain.

Achieving Consensus

How do you achieve consensus without having access to a centralized database? Who will control the database without a central authority which tracks balances and accounts and transactions?

Until Satoshi came forward with the solution, nobody even believed that such a thing was possible.

So, now we can move forward with the meaning and definition of cryptocurrencies. Without any additional technical brouhaha, a cryptocurrency is simply an entry in a particular database that you cannot change until you have complied with specific conditions as laid down in the database governance. Surprised? Well, this is how your bank account works too.

Your account is nothing but a string of entries that are centrally stored and you can alter these entries only under specific conditions including the condition that you actually possess the entries and the subsequent balance in your account.

So, money or currency is nothing but a string of entries in a central database that has details of accounts, transactions and balances.

How to create, mine, and confirm transactions using cryptocurrency

Let me illustrate the working of cryptocurrency with an example. Firstly, cryptocurrency is so-called upon because the consensus among the users is achieved through cryptography.
Suppose Peter gives X bitcoins to Harry. There will be a transaction created which is essentially a file that contains the transaction details. In this case, the transaction file or block will contain. "Peter gives X bitcoins to Harry." This block will be signed by Peter using his private key.

When the block is signed, it is broadcasted across the P2P network resulting in every node or computer being updated with this transaction. The transaction will be recognized by every peer in the network immediately but it will get confirmed only after a specified time period. Confirmation of transactions is the key element in cryptocurrency.

Until the confirmation for a transaction does happen, it remains open to changes and forgery. Once, the confirmation is completed, then it is like being cast in stone and neither will changes be allowed nor will they be forgettable. The transaction in the form of a block will become an irreversible historical record that is attached to the Blockchain.

The users who confirm transactions in cryptocurrency are called *miners*. They look at the transaction and give them a legitimate stamp. These legitimized blocks are then added to all the nodes and become a part of the complete blockchain.

Miners get rewarded or paid with tokens like bitcoins for the work they do. Since miners play such an important role in cryptocurrency it makes sense to spend some time understanding their function.

Miners

Technically any node in the blockchain network can be a miner. This is because there is an absence of centralized control to delegate tasks. However, for the express purpose of preventing misuse and abuse of the cryptocurrency legacy, it was imperative that a robust mechanism exists that keeps strong and powerful checks on such abuse and misuse.

Without this checking mechanism (decentralized though it might be), it is possible that someone can create numerous of peers in the P2P network and create forged transactions. So, transactions have to be vetted and confirmed by people who know how to do it.

Rules Of A Miner

So, Satoshi Nakamoto laid rules for anyone who wishes to become a miner. The potential miner will have to invest some amount of work so that they can qualify as miners. Miners need to find the hash that matches the block under consideration to the previous block in the Blockchain. This "hash" is a cryptographic function and is the proof-of-work. Bitcoin cryptocurrency uses the SHA 256 Hash algorithm for transaction confirmations.
The SHA 256 is the foundation of a cryptographic puzzle that miners compete with each other to solve. Once the miner finds the solution to this puzzle, the block will be added

to the Blockchain and the miner will receive an incentive in the form of bitcoins.

Only when a miner solves this cryptographic puzzle, can a transaction block become valid. And the difficulty of this puzzle increases with the increase in the number of nodes in the network. Thus, only a specific number of blocks (that translate to cryptocurrency) can be created and mined in any given period of time.

Properties Of Cryptocurrencies

The transactions are irreversible. Once, the confirmation of a transaction is done by a miner, it becomes cast in stone and can never be reversed by anyone.

Only the pseudonyms are known and recognized. You can track the transaction flow but it is *not possible* to connect the identity of the users in the real world.

The transactions happen almost instantaneously and are global in nature. It does not matter when you choose to make the payment to your neighbor or someone in another part of the globe. The transaction time and confirmation details are independent of geography.

The transactions are extremely secure as they are confirmed based on the system of public key cryptography. Only a user who has a private key can transmit cryptocurrency through the system. A powerful cryptographic system combined with the magical number of large numbers make it computationally unfeasible to crack or hack into the system.

There is no gatekeeper to the cryptocurrency system and anyone can join. It is downloadable software that can be used by all for free.

There is a controlled supply of tokens in any cryptocurrency system. In the Bitcoin system, tokens are available till the final token is used up somewhere in 2140. The currency supply decreases with time.

Cryptocurrencies are like money in the form of gold. This is quite in contrast to the money you hold in your account which works like a debt. The present banking system works like an I.O.U.

Potential effects of cryptocurrencies on the present banking system
Cryptocurrencies are pseudonymous, permission-less and irreversible. This approach to money and monetary policies can attack the

present banking and financial systems of the world. Citizens' money is presently controlled by this system and any change in policy can affect the value of your asset.

There is a controlled and limited supply of tokens in a cryptocurrency system that is outside the control of any government or financial institution. This approach takes away the control of any centralized power point to affect inflation and/or deflation by controlling the supply of money in the system.

Cryptocurrencies with their revolutionary approach to managing and handling money have the power to be the start of a new economic order in the world.

Chapter 4: Blockchain Technology In Social Media

While the first application of Blockchain technology developed by Satoshi Nakamoto was in cryptocurrency, today, this amazing technology has spread its wings and soared to other worlds as well. This chapter is dedicated to the use of Blockchain technology in the field of social media with specific reference to Steemit.

Steemit is a blockchain powered social media network that was launched in March 2016. Steemit is developed by Daniel Larimer and Ned Scott. While the former is the founder of BitShares, a decentralized exchange for share trading, the latter is a financial analyst.

Steemit has been developed as a social media network to allow people to create and post content. The blockchain technology that Larimer used to build Steemit is called Graphene. Graphene allows for developing and deploying blockchains that are specific to an application.

Social Media That Pays You

The most explosive aspect of Steemit is the concept of paying people who contributed blogs and posts and to those who voted on blogs and posts through this social media platform.

During the initial months of the launch, Steemit only saw a few miners who contributed content. Then, what happened on 4th July 2016 changed the way Steemit was perceived.

Until this date, people who were promised that they will be paid for creating blogs, posts, and upvotes would get paid actually got their money. The rewards for the posts on the social media blockchain were given out on 4th July 2016.

So how does it work exactly? Steemit works like a blogging social media site that pays you. It's like Reddit but you get paid every time you post something and the amount you get paid determines how popular your posts. Other Steemit users or steemers will vote on your post. Kind of like a thumbs up and thumbs down system. The more thumbs up you have, the more you will get paid. The more comments and interactions you have with people, the more your posts are worth, the more your profile is perceived as relevant, and ultimately, you can actually earn hard cash with this system in place.

Think of about this possibility. You create a post about something that went viral. You put pictures, videos, opinions, write a well-written article about it, interact with others, and next thing you know you've made a few dollars. Check back a day later and you might just get lucky and made $10,000 with that one post. Sounds farfetched right? That's when your wrong. There are PLENTY of people that are actually making a good living of Steemit.

Of course, it takes time to become established, but once you get there, it could be actually a very lucrative hobby.

Futhermore, the SEO significance of Steemit on Google and other search engines have really changed the social media game. More on this later. For now, let's investigate some aspects of Steemit.

What Is Steem?

The core of Steemit is Steem, the cryptocurrency that is very similar to Bitcoin. Like all other cryptocurrencies, Steem is fungible, transferable and freely movable. Yet, this cryptocurrency is available in two different forms under two different smart contracts.

The two forms of Steem smart contracts are *Steem Power* and *Steem Dollar*. Depending on your need, you can sign the smart contract for Steem Power or Steem Dollar.

Steem Power – offers leverage as well as utility. Steem Power adds power to your vote. That means to say, the more Steem Power you have, the stronger your vote is on the Steemit platform.

Steemit Power is a way to encourage users to remain committed to the platform for a longer period of time With Steem Power, you will be able to invest your money immediately but you are expected to wait for some time to get returns on your investment.

Steem Power smart contracts can be compared to what venture capitalists do. Steem Power can be converted based to Steem, the base currency, through 104 weekly conversions.

Steem Dollars – This works like a debt instrument. The token holder is promised $1 worth of Steem at a future date, but after a seven-day conversion process. This gap of seven days is to prevent arbitrage transactions wherein someone who has an advantage of a price difference will not be able to earn more than the $1 that is intended by the smart contract.

Steem Dollars works exactly like a debt instrument inasmuch that this smart contract will not be able to leverage any value increase of Steem. So, for example, if Steem was worth $1, then the individual holding Steem Dollars will also receive one Steem for every Steem Dollar he or she owned. However, if the worth of one Steem went up to $2, then the holder of Steem Dollars will receive 0.5 Steem for every Steem Dollar he or she owns.

The lock-in period is compensated by an interest payment that is set at the time of signing the Steem Dollar smart contract.

How to earn rewards (or Steem) on Steemit?
There are two ways to earn rewards on Steem namely writing a blog post and by voting for a good post. Individuals creating good quality content gets paid and individuals giving votes to posts and blogs also get paid. Every day, Steemit currency units are newly created and distributed to the people who engage on their social media platform. So, the more you engage, the more you can get paid.

Why this is a game changer?

Because Steemit is so new and so enticing, we are people making a ton of money with Steemit. The future of all social medias could be funnled into this system of paying for quality content. For this reason alone, Google has adopted a process in which rewards Steemit users; not necessarily by money but in SEO.

Steemit and SEO

SEO or search engine optimization is a term in which can be explained simply as, how your website or anything in the web can be ranked in a search engine like Google. Believe it not, you use this everyday. If you ever want to "google" something, you go onto Google and look for information based on that keyword.

Realistically, people will search in pages 1 or 2 in Google for whatever they're looking for. For example, you want to know what are the best deals for laptops during Black Friday this year in November. Usually you would google "Black Friday lap top deals" and see what comes up. Furthermore, it's most likely you only search pages 1,2, or 3 and if you can't find what you're looking for, you would probably change the search term.

Because profitable websites highly dependent on ranking in the top page or second page in Google, SEO now becomes a priority. So how can companies, bloggers, websites, forums, or anyone with web content want to monetize their websites better, all the while by competing with millions of related searches? Well that's where Steemit comes in.

Believe it or not, if you write an article on Steemit and include links, photos, videos, and other quality content, Google will reward your website much higher than other websites because it's on Steemit. This is because Google has included Steemit in its algorithm as a highly reputable website. It views it as a highly reputable website because Steemit ties in *currency* to your blog posts. Whenever Google sees that you are getting paid some cash for a post you made on Steemit, they are essentially saying to themselves, "highly monetizable content, let's push it to the top of the search results in Google." That right there is a game-changer when it comes to selling things online and leap frogging the competition when it comes to SEO.

Payment for content creators – As a content creator, you must endeavor to get more number of votes for your posts and blogs. It is important to remember here that all votes do not have the same voting power. Here are some of the ways votes can have different powers and values:

For instance, if two people voted for the same post and one had 10,000 Steem Power and the other had 1,000 Steem Power, then the latter's votes have more value than the former's. This has led many content creators to chase big-value votes by trying to convince big Steem Power holders to vote for their content. In fact, if any of the founders (Ned Scott or Daniel Larimer) voted for any of the posts, then there is a huge hike in the value of the particular post.

Moreover, votes from large Steem Power holders bring in more votes from others too.

Payment for voters - Now, for people earning rewards by giving upvotes, Steemit works like this. If a post that you have voted for does well, then you earn more than another post, which does not do so well. This approach of incentivizing ensures that you give your vote only to those posts that you truly believe are of high quality.

Another interesting point about votes for posts is that if you chose to vote for more than one post, then your second vote loses value depending on the time that has lapsed between the two votes. Essentially, multiple votes from the same account results in the reduction of the value of each subsequent vote.

Proof-Of-Work In Steemit

A security-less Blockchain has no value as no one will have faith in the system. The proof-of-stake algorithm for Steemit is taken from the BitShares project that Daniel Larimer developed.

Steemit uses a delegated proof-of-work algorithm. This form of proof-of-work algorithm entails the community to vote for "witnesses" who will become responsible for verifying and confirming transactions. Witnesses are the miners in Steemit.

The system of delegation can be comparable to a democratic republic way of voting for Congressmen on whom the voters place the responsibility to govern the country. In the delegated proof-of-stake algorithm, the community chooses witnesses who will be responsible for keeping the network safe and secure.

It is important to remember here that if witnesses do not do their jobs correctly, then they can be and are replaced with a better worker by the community.

There is a total of 21 witnesses responsible for verifying and confirming blocks each time a block is created. From this list of 21, 19 are voted for in the manner described above. The 20th is a random witness who may not have made it to the top 19 and the 21st witness is a typical miner performing the typical proof-of-work confirmations. This combination of witnesses is formed so as to provide the Blockchain technology based Steemit social media platform the most reliable form of verifications and confirmations.

The Future Of Steemit

Despite the presence of skeptics, Steemit is growing in popularity. The three currency units of Steem, Steem Power, and Steem Dollar continue to attract new users every day to the platform. While the social media itself is attracting hundreds of users daily, Blockchain technologists are also creating plenty of software to track vote-chasing users, to sell and buy goods on Steemit, etc.

You can read umpteen stories of successful Steemit earners. Whether the excitement will be lasting or not is for time to tell. But, as of now, Steemit is a highly popular and trendy social media platform that is powered by Blockchain technology.

Chapter 5: Banks And Financial Institutions With Blockchain Technology Products

As Blockchain technology is slowly gaining ground in the financial segment of the world, many banks and financial institutions are also investing resources to research and create customer-centric products using this technology. This chapter gives you a bird's view of the various banks and financial institutions and the various Blockchain technology-based products they are creating for their customers.

NASDAQ – In May 2015, NASDAQ made an announcement that they are looking at Blockchain technology to enhance their scalability and capability specifically on its Private Market Platform. This NASDAQ platform, started in January 2014, allows for pre-IPO trading amongst private companies. NASDAQ announced a partnership deal that it signed with Chain, a provider of Blockchain technology for FIs and banks for this purpose.

Deutsche Bank – is exploring options to use Blockchain technology for paying and settling fiat currencies and asset registries. The bank is also looking to leverage the power of Blockchain technology for its derivative contracts, AML and KYC registries, for regulatory reporting, etc. The German bank has been researching Blockchain technology for such activities in its labs in the Silicon Valley, London, and Berlin as per a July 2015 report.

EBA – As per a report released by Euro Banking Association (EBA) in May 2015, it was exploring and studying the effects of Blockchain technology on the payment and banking scenario in the next 1-3 years. In the report, EBA confirmed taking note of how this technology can be used by banks to cut down audit and governance costs, to provide improved and secure products and to decrease time to market as well.

DBS Bank – This Singapore-based bank has organized and conducted Blockchain hackathons in May 2015 in collaboration with Startupbootcamp, FinTech, and Coin Republic. The latter is a bitcoin company based in Singapore. These events sponsored by banks reflect the interest that Blockchain technology is generating in the banking sector.

US Federal Reserve – As per a March 2015 report, the US Federal Reserve is purportedly working with IBM to develop a Blockchain technology-based digital payment system.
Standard Chartered Bank – As per a LinkedIn post by the then CIO (Chief Innovation Officer) of SCB, the bank is working on a system

powered by Blockchain technology to improve transparencies in banking transactions and to cut costs.

LHV Bank – This bank has reportedly started work on Blockchain technology-based systems such as an app called Cuber Wallet that uses colored coins. LHV Bank is also collaborating with two Blockchain technology companies such as Coinfloor and Coinbase. The bank is working on creating a digital security system based on blockchain technology.

Fidor Bank – has collaborated with Kraken to build a digital currency exchange in the European Union. The bank also collaborated with Ripple Labs to offer money transfer services using Blockchain technology.

Barclays Bank – has two labs in London that are open for conducting Blockchain technology experiments by coders, businesses, and entrepreneurs in the field. Barclays has collaborated with Safello to develop multiple Blockchain powered banking services.

Similarly, ANZ Bank, BNP Paribas, and USAA Bank are working with different Blockchain technology companies exploring options that they could use in mainstream banking channels.

Citibank – One of the world's largest banks, Citibank has set up multiple systems to research and deploy systems powered by Blockchain technology. Citibank has developed "citicoin," a cryptocurrency that is used internally to understand the working cryptocurrencies better.

It is becoming evident that Blockchain technology is catching the interest of large banks, financial institutions, and trading exchanges. There is a lot of experimental work going on wherein commodities such as diamond, gold, and silver can also be brought into the Blockchain technology realm.

Concepts are being worked on to create systems based on Blockchain technology to help in elections, to establish ownership of real-estate properties, etc.

There are numerous companies worldwide that are offering Blockchain technology applications for a variety of purposes for both financial and non-financial needs.

In the banking and finance sector, the areas where Blockchain technology is catching the attention of the leaders include remittances and trading platforms. Many banks want to send and receive money faster, in a more secure manner, and with reduced costs as compared to the present system that they are using. Similarly, trading platforms are very encouraging about using Blockchain technology.

Even in non-financial uses, Blockchain technology is slowly surely gaining ground. Many companies are keen on using the smart contracts offered by Blockchain technology. Companies creating and maintaining smart contracts are getting a lot of funding from investors.

Blockchain technology, thus, seems to have caught the fancy of multiple players in the financial segment and a few players in the non-financial segment as well.

Chapter 6: Benefits And Limitations Of Blockchain Technology

Like I said in the beginning, many technological experts believe that it is likely Blockchain technology has the power to become the next revolution after the Internet. Just like the worldwide web, Blockchain technology can disrupt the conventional working and operations of certain industries and with time and effort, the technology has the potential to take on the entire world by storm.

Thus, it is quite natural that entities and individuals favoring the outcome of this technology and those who are not in favor are at butting heads with each other. Moreover, like most things in the world, Blockchain technology too has a range of benefits and also a range of limitations that need to be worked on before it is able to reach its full potential.

This chapter is dedicated to studying and understanding the benefits and limitations of Blockchain technology.

Benefits Of Blockchain Technology

No need for an intermediary between related parties – Blockchain technology allows two parties to make an exchange without the need of any third-party intermediary to oversee the exchange process. And this exchange takes place without any risk to any of the parties concerned.

Users are highly empowered – All users in the Blockchain are completely empowered to control all aspects of the exchange and their own privacy as well.

The data that is distributed is of high quality – The data in the blockchain is consistent, complete, accurate, timely, and is also widely distributed.

Longevity, Reliability, and Durability – As there is no centralized version of the information in Blockchain technology, the system will not have any core point of failure. This increases its ability to withstand malicious attacks making the data more durable and reliable and the entire system more sustainable than the conventional centralized information points of today.

The integrity of data is achieved through the process itself – the integrity of the transactions on a Blockchain is achieved through the process itself. That is to say, transactions are executed as per the existing protocols that are put in place and hence there is no need for a third party assessor.

Transactions on a Blockchain are immutable – Once a transaction is confirmed on a Blockchain, it becomes immutable and cannot be changed or altered or deleted.

Transactions are highly transparent – Transactions in a Blockchain are highly transparent as all parties can view them.

The ecosystem is highly simplified – As all the transactions are added to a single public ledger, there is no need to maintain multiple ledgers and records resulting in a simple ecosystem doing away with the complexities and clutter of multiple ledger systems.

Financial transactions can happen much faster than in the conventional banking system – Money transfers between banks across different countries can take days in the present conventional banking system. With Blockchain technology, this time period can reduce drastically resulting in faster transactions and transfers.

Transaction costs are lower – The elimination of third party intermediary and the associated overhead costs brings down the overall transaction costs in Blockchain technology powered systems. It works both ways in both the front and end user. Fees are typically the shard side of the sword that consumers don't like. By eliminating a third party, seamless transactions can occur, and accountability ultimately falls in the service; not on a third party or consumer.

Limitations Of Blockchain Technology

It is a very nascent technology – Blockchain technology is just about raising its head in the commercial aspects of the human world. It is still in the rudimentary stages of development. Challenges such as scalability of data limits, transaction speeds, and the veracity of the verification process are all yet to be tested in systems that handle large volumes 24/7.

The regulatory status of Blockchain technology is still uncertain – As of now, currencies are regulated and controlled by the government. Such kind of regulatory control or regulation does not exist for Blockchain technology and hence is not easily accepted by financial institutions. The next chapter deals with the legality aspect of Blockchain technology in detail.

There is a need for huge computational power - Presently, a miner in the Blockchain needs a huge amount of computational power to try nearly 450 thousand trillion solutions every second to validate or confirm transactions on the Blockchain. This kind of computational power is really stupendous and thus could be a big limitation when we need a large number of transactions confirmed and approved continually such as in large banking scenario.

Fear of privacy, control, and security – Despite reassurances that Blockchain technology is computationally unfeasible to hack into and thus privacy, control, and security will not be compromised, certain cyber security issues still need to be addressed before people find the confidence to hand over personal data to Blockchain technology-supported systems.

There are many integration concerns that exist in Blockchain technology – In order to implement products based on Blockchain technology, the existing systems require a lot of changes or need to be replaced entirely which could deter companies from accepting these solutions. Companies need to strategize their transitions slowly and over a long period of time.

There is a paradigm shift to decentralized systems – A paradigm shift in outlook is required from both operators and users to change from centralized systems to decentralized systems. It could take some time for this kind of cultural adoption to happen across the world.

High initial costs – While transaction costs are bound to come down in the future, initial capital costs are quite high and can be a deterrent for many companies.

Despite these challenges, there are multiple companies spread across the world, which are investing time and resources to work on solutions that are powered by Blockchain technology. Here is a small list of companies that are into Blockchain technology working on providing solutions for various applications:

Companies providing solutions for storing and delivering digital content and documents

Blockcai
BitProof
ArtPlus
Ascribe
Chainy.Link
Blocktech
Stampery

Blockparti
BlockCDN
The Rudimental

Companies providing solutions for authentication and authorization

The Real McCoy
Degree of Trust
Everpass
BlockVerify
Companies providing digital identity solutions
Sho Card
Uniquid
Onename
Trustatom

Companies providing smart contracts solutions
Otonomos
Mirror
Symbiont

Chapter 7: Legality Issues In Blockchain Technology

As Blockchain technology is becoming more widespread and increasing in popularity across various industries, there are legality issues that are cropping up and need to be addressed on an ongoing basis. A robust legal framework is the backbone of trust and user-confidence in any new system.

This chapter is dedicated to giving you some of these legal impediments that need to be overcome before Blockchain technology can be accepted more wholeheartedly accepted by the general public.

Financial transfers – Today, digital currencies are being used as mediums of exchange and as speculative investments. It is highly feasible to use Blockchain technology to perform speedier and more secure financial transfers such as global remittances, currency exchanges, settlement and clearing of payments, and interbank transfers. However, before this technology is brought into mainstream financial markets and the banking sector, Blockchain technology needs to be incorporated into the present set of financial regulatory system so that any potential disputes can be amicably settled under law.

Transactions requiring multiple signatures would need to be redefined in the financial regulatory system – Blockchain technology does support transactions that need multiple signatures. An example of such a transaction is that of an escrow account, which is in the center of three parties including the two contracting parties and an "escrow account party" which will be the third party. Refunding the money lying in the escrow account requires two of the three parties to sign off.

The existing laws governing the physical control of escrow accounts cannot suffice for transactions done via blockchain technology systems. This is because, in these systems, there is nothing physical to be delivered or controlled. Hence, new laws have to be written for such multi-signature transactions.

Colored coins or merchant-issued currencies have little or no regulatory control - Such currencies are very blurred in the present regulatory system. Colored coins or merchant-issued currencies can be given as gift cards and/or discount coupons, which can be redeemed by purchasing products at the merchants. For example, a merchant could give the value of a bitcoin in the form of a $500 voucher that can be used to pay while buying products from the merchant. However, the value of the bitcoin remains the same. Hence, resulting product ends up getting dual credit creating double entries for the same bitcoin that will lead to disputes and confusions. These types of transactions need further study before being brought into the mainstream.

Issues in intellectual property – Blockchain technology will be able to offer a low-cost and secure medium to track and record intellectual property. However, legal systems need to undergo paradigm shift before implementing the systems in the general public arena. The present legal system focuses on the contract between the buyer and seller, which can then be sold further down. However, with Blockchain technology-based systems, there could arise issues that are applicable in case of digital products. For example, in the case of a first sale, a purchaser who has bought the property can sell it to someone else.

However, with digital files, the problem lies in the fact that it is difficult or impossible to determine whether the first reseller (or the original purchaser) sold the original file to the second purchaser or only a copy of the original file. In Blockchain technology, this problem can be overcome as digital copies can be verified and confirmed individually so that sellers transfer the full rights of the original file. However, these have to be incorporated into our regulatory system before Blockchain technology becomes implementable in the intellectual property market.

Issues in data transfer and storage – Blockchain technology allows you to create systems to transfer and store data digitally in a decentralized manner. For example, identity data can be easily stored and verified through a Blockchain ledger keeping the original identity safe from theft and offering anonymity in the form of a digital pseudonym.

However, such verifications could raise worries whether privacy is possible in such systems. Moreover, when you create large data repositories, concerns of a breach will always linger. Despite the fact that cryptographic ledgers are perceived as being very secure and private, there could be a possibility that personal information from another source is exposed and if that can be related to this Blockchain then privacy concerns will become genuine and not a mere fear factor of a technically ignorant individual.

Additionally, it is possible that data from Blockchains are collected and analyzed by a powerful computing device. If such a thing happens, then these transactions or blocks can be easily tracked and identified in spite of being in a pseudonymous ledger system. Thus, these identity and data thefts are a cause for concern when dealing with transferring and storing data through Blockchain technology systems.

Legal issues with smart contracts – As you already know by now, smart contracts are one of the core principles of Blockchain technology. Smart contracts are programmed arrangements that are automatically enforced upon the user and are self-executing in nature.

These contracts exist only in the online mode and help in making payments in social media platforms such as Steemit or to sell digital goods through activation codes that are activated (through Blockchain technology systems) only after payment is received for the goods.

However, smart contracts do have some unanswered legal issues. The primary cause for concern is the fact that it is automatically enforced. This aspect is in complete contrast to the classic contract laws that require a deliberate approval from the user before being enforced. Smart contracts are quite possibly not cancellable or voidable thereby making it an unconscionable and coerced contract.

A second cause of concern is related to the privacy aspect of Blockchain technology. Any contract between two parties will be able on the Blockchain for public viewing and thus, third parties could potentially track and take undue advantage by watching the movement of the contract.

Issues with decentralized organization of Blockchain technology – While the freedom from having to depend on a third-party centralized repository holder can reduce costs and undue interference, a major concern with regard to this kind of approach is how to raise and manage liability issues that crop up in the transaction. Who will be ultimately responsible for smooth functioning of the entire system? Who can be held responsible if any law is broken? In the same way, legal status of the entities will also in question.

Issue of securities through Blockchain technology – There have been companies that have developed and used Blockchain technology to issue securities to the general public. Companies have also raised funds through sale of securities in the form of native tokens though these sales have been given the profile not so much as company securities but rather as sales to access technology.

Whether all tokens can be treated securities cannot have a simple answer. The answer is dependent on multiple factors including but not limited to the process and other aspects of the sale and the clauses in the smart contracts. As these choices are new in the market, regulators and exchange controllers will have to sit down and formulate new laws or change old ones to incorporate these novels yet not fully explored technological advances.

Legal Issues and Blockchain technology: the way forward -

While legal issues are being fought out and new changes are being made to the legal framework, it is an undeniable fact that Blockchain technology will not stop generating interest among users and operators. Blockchain technology can change the way we do business and exchange data and goods in the market.

It is quite possible that an entirely new segment in the legal framework may be created to fit in the new possibilities and innovations that Blockchain technology offers to us. Yes, legal issues will continue to be at the core of this technology. Yet, the absence of an ideal legal framework should not deter users, operators, and technological experts from trying to explore new opportunities in this realm.

Conclusion

Blockchain technology gets its name from the concept of cryptographic blocks that are employed to validate and confirm transactions. The validated blocks are linked together to form a chain ad hence the name Blockchain technology. The data in the Blockchain is accessible to everyone who has access to a copy of it. However, no one can change or alter or delete any data or blocks in the chain.

Blocks are validated by solving cryptographic puzzles that become increasingly complex as the number of nodes increases in the Blockchain network. When the puzzle is solved, the block gets validated and becomes an immutable part of the Blockchain. The people who solve these puzzles are called miners who get rewarded for their work of solving the puzzle and validating the blocks.

In this concluding chapter, let us summarize the key components of Blockchain technology.

Distributed database – Blockchain technology works on the concept of a distributed database wherein all the information and data are held in multiple copies across computers or nodes connected through a network. This information is continually updated and reconciled all through the multiple copies.

Blockchain technology offers durability and robustness – There are inbuilt durability and robustness properties in systems created with Blockchain technology. This is because the Blockchain is not controlled by any one single entity and has no one particular point of failure making it nearly impossible for hackers to get in.

Blockchain technology is incorruptible and transparent – The data is embedded in the system and is available for public viewing and hence is highly transparent. It would require an immensely huge amount of computing power to corrupt a Blockchain hence making it computational unfeasible to corrupt it.

Blockchain technology uses a network of computing nodes to make up the Blockchain - Each node gets a copy of the Blockchain which gets automatically downloaded when you join the Blockchain.

Blockchain technology promotes a decentralized concept – The technology works on data being decentralized and available as multiple copies in all the connected nodes. This decentralized concept enhances the security of the data as there is no one point of vulnerability that can be broken to get all the data.

Blockchain technology uses encryption technology for protection – While the traditional computing system using usernames and passwords for identity protection, Blockchain technology uses encryption keys for protection. It uses a combination of public and private keys to embed data securely in a block before adding it to the parent block.

Blockchain technology brings a new layer into the Internet's functionality – While bitcoins and other cryptocurrencies are already popular among users who are transacting directly with each other, there could be additional financial segments such as clearing and settlement, KYC and AML monitoring, and data management that could use the power of Blockchain technology.

Blockchain technology can have immense potential in myriad applications and is not just limited to cryptocurrencies and banking products. Some of the non-financial uses of Blockchain technology include:
• To set up decentralized trading exchanges

- To set up distributed cloud storage systems

- To track and manage digital identity in a safe and secure way as in the case of passport issuance and management, E-residency, birth certificates, wedding certificates, etc

- To track and manage digital voting systems

- To record and track data through a safe record-keeping mechanism

- The concept of Blockchain technology is still evolving and new applications are being discovered continually.

Despite legal hurdles and other teething problems that are part of any new technology, many experts are of the firm belief that Blockchain technology has the potential to change the way the world does business and communicate with each other. Many technological experts called it the Blockchain revolution and not merely Blockchain technology!

I hope this book has given you sufficient reason to learn more and understand the concept of Blockchain technology better. So, go ahead and take that important to leverage the power of a new and yet untapped technology and see what opportunities it can bring to you!

Resources

https://hackernoon.com/explaining-blockchain-how-proof-of-work-enables-trustless-consensus-2abed27f0845#.oprr3oi2v

http://www.coindesk.com/steemit-blockchain-social-media-how-works/

http://blockgeeks.com/guides/what-is-cryptocurrency

https://letstalkpayments.com/an-overview-of-blockchain-technology/

https://www.financierworldwide.com/legal-implications-of-expanded-use-of-blockchain-technology/#.WMZu-NR96t8

Related Titles

Hacking University: Freshman Edition Essential Beginner's Guide on How to Become an Amateur Hacker

Hacking University: Sophomore Edition. Essential Guide to Take Your Hacking Skills to the Next Level. Hacking Mobile Devices, Tablets, Game Consoles, and Apps

Hacking University: Junior Edition. Learn Python Computer Programming From Scratch. Become a Python Zero to Hero. The Ultimate Beginners Guide in Mastering the Python Language

Hacking University: Senior Edition Linux. Optimal Beginner's Guide To Precisely Learn And Conquer The Linux Operating System. A Complete Step By Step Guide In How Linux Command Line Works

Hacking University: Graduation Edition. 4 Manuscripts (Computer, Mobile, Python, & Linux). Hacking Computers, Mobile Devices, Apps, Game Consoles and Learn Python & Linux

Data Analytics: Practical Data Analysis and Statistical Guide to Transform and Evolve Any Business, Leveraging the power of Data Analytics, Data Science, and Predictive Analytics for Beginners

About the Author

Isaac D. Cody is a proud, savvy, and ethical hacker from New York City. After receiving a Bachelors of Science at Syracuse University, Isaac now works for a mid-size Informational Technology Firm in the heart of NYC. He aspires to work for the United States government as a security hacker, but also loves teaching others about the future of technology. Isaac firmly believes that the future will heavily rely computer "geeks" for both security and the successes of companies and future jobs alike. In his spare time, he loves to analyze and scrutinize everything about the game of basketball.

www.ingramcontent.com/pod-product-compliance
Lightning Source LLC
Chambersburg PA
CBHW061200180526
45170CB00002B/893